ANIMAL DETECTIVES / DETECTIVES DEL REINO ANIMAL

# BEDBUG-SNIFFING BEAGLES
## and Other Scent Hounds

# BEAGLES CAZADORES DE CHINCHES
## y otros sabuesos

### Rosie Albright

Traducción al español: Eduardo Alamán

**PowerKiDS**
press

New York

Published in 2012 by The Rosen Publishing Group, Inc.
29 East 21st Street, New York, NY 10010

First Edition

Editor: Joanne Randolph                    Traducción al español: Eduardo Alamán
Book Design: Kate Laczynski

Photo Credits: Cover, pp. 9, 18, 22 Stan Honda/AFP/Getty Images; pp. 4–5 Philipp Guelland/ AFP/Getty Images; pp. 6, 24 (airport) Shutterstock.com; p. 10 Karen Kasmauski/Getty Images; p. 13 Brian Kersey/Getty Images; pp. 14–15 Visuals Unlimited, Inc./Alex Wild/Getty Images; pp. 17, 24 (mattresses) Justin Sullivan/Getty Images; p. 21 Fuse/Getty Images; p. 24 (blood) © www.iStockphoto.com/wellglad; p. 24 (couch) © www.iStockphoto.com/Justin Allfree.

Library of Congress Cataloging-in-Publication Data

Albright, Rosie.
   [Bedbug-sniffing beagles and other scent hounds. Spanish & English]
   Bedbug-sniffing beagles and other scent hounds = Beagles cazadores de chinches y otros sabuesos / by Rosie Albright. — 1st ed.
      p. cm. — (Animal detectives = Detectives del reino animal)
   Includes index.
   ISBN 978-1-4488-6726-4 (library binding)
   1. Beagle (Dog breed)—Juvenile literature. 2. Hounds—Juvenile literature. 3. Bedbugs— Juvenile literature. I. Title. II. Title: Beagles cazadores de chinches y otros sabuesos.
   SF429.B3A4318 2012
   636.753′70886—dc23

                                   2011027099

**Web Sites**: Due to the changing nature of Internet links, PowerKids Press has developed an online list of Web sites related to the subject of this book. This site is updated regularly. Please use this link to access the list:
www.powerkidslinks.com/andt/bedbug/

Manufactured in the United States of America

CPSIA Compliance Information: Batch #WW12PK: For Further Information contact Rosen Publishing, New York, New York at 1-800-237-9932

# CONTENTS

# CONTENIDO

Beagles have been used as hunting dogs for many years. They mainly hunt rabbits.

Durante años, los beagles se han usado para la cacería. Principalmente, los beagles cazan liebres.

Beagles are well-loved family pets, too. President Lyndon B. Johnson had three beagles named Him, Her, and Edgar.

---

Además los beagles son buenas mascotas. El presidente Lyndon B. Johnson tenía tres beagles, llamados, Él, Ella y Edgar.

Beagles are part of a group called scent hounds. They have a great sense of smell.

---

Los beagles pertenecen a la familia de los sabuesos. Los sabuesos tienen un gran sentido del olfato.

10

A government group called the USDA uses beagles. Their Beagle Brigade sniffs out illegal produce at **airports**.

---

El grupo del gobierno llamado USDA usa a los beagles. Esta Brigada de Beagles olfatea productos ilegales en los **aeropuertos**.

Beagles are trained to find bedbugs. Trainers put bedbugs in cans to teach beagles what they smell like.

---

Los beagles se entrenan para encontrar chinches. Los entrenadores ponen chinches en latas para que conozcan su olor.

14

Bedbugs are small bugs that feed on people's **blood**. They eat at night.

---

Las chinches son insectos pequeños que se alimentan de la **sangre** de las personas. Las chinches comen de noche.

Trained beagles find bedbugs living in **mattresses**. Bedbugs are flat, brown, and wingless.

Los beagles encuentran chinches en los **colchones**. Las chinches son de color marrón, planas y sin alas.

17

Beagles can find bedbugs in **couches**. Bedbugs hide in small, dark places.

---

Los beagles pueden encontrar chinches en los **sillones**. Las chinches se esconden en lugares pequeños y oscuros.

Bloodhounds and other scent hounds are used to find bedbugs, too.

Los perros de San Huberto, y otros sabuesos, también se usan para encontrar chinches.

Beagles and other scent hounds use their noses to help people.

---

Los beagles y otros sabuesos usan sus narices para ayudar a las personas.

# Words to Know / Palabras que debes saber

airport / (el) aeropuerto

blood / (la) sangre

couch / (el) sillón

mattress / (el) colchón